Sea Killers

by David Orme

Ransom

Trailblazers

Sea Killers
by David Orme
Educational consultant: Helen Bird

Illustrated by Demitri Nezis

Published by Ransom Publishing Ltd.
Rose Cottage, Howe Hill, Watlington, Oxon. OX49 5HB
www.ransom.co.uk

ISBN   184167 592 X

        978 184167 592 3

First published in 2006

Sea Killers

Contents

Sea
killers

Get
the
facts

Sea killers file 1: Sharks

There are about 350 types of shark in the world.

Only a few of them attack people.

These are the most
dangerous:

Bull shark
Great white shark
Tiger shark

*Great white
shark*

*Tiger
shark*

How not to get eaten

Keep a look-out. One fin is probably a dolphin. Two fins is a shark!

Swim in the middle of the day when sharks are not feeding.

Don't wear bright colours or carry shiny things.

If you see a shark . . .

Stay calm. Swim calmly and quietly back to the shore.

Don't shout or wave your arms.

How likely is a shark attack?

Not very. Fewer than 100 people are attacked each year, with only about 20 deaths.

Some types of shark are becoming extinct because of fishing. *Sharks need protecting from people!*

Sea killers file 2: Deadly creatures

Stone Fish

This is a **stone fish**. They look like stones so people sometimes tread on them.

The spines on their backs can go right through a shoe. The poison causes **terrible pain** which can last for a long time.

People who have not been treated quickly have had feet amputated.

There is only one thing worse than stepping on a stonefish – *and that's sitting on one*.

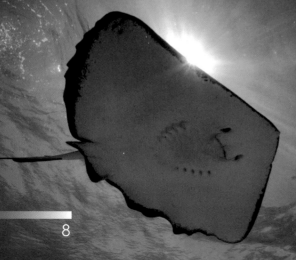

Stingray

The sting from a **stingray** can be deadly.

Luckily they are scared of people and will swim away if there are people near.

The blue-ringed octopus

This is a very tiny creature. It is the size of a golf ball. It looks harmless – but its bite can **kill**.

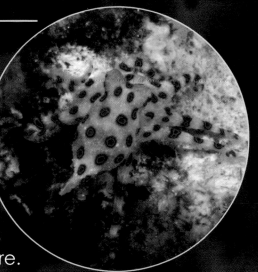

Its poison is more powerful than the deadliest snake.

If you are bitten, you will be paralysed in minutes. **Death is almost certain** – there is no cure.

Jellyfish

Some jellyfish make you itch if you touch them. Some will kill you.

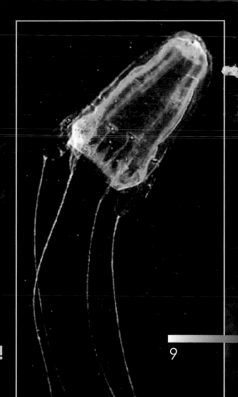

The most deadly is the Chironex. It is also called the **wasp fish** or **box jellyfish**.

A touch with just a short piece of tentacle will cause terrible pain. The tentacles stick to your skin. The poison will kill you quickly.

The Chironex causes around 70 deaths a year.

So - stay away from these critters!

Sea killers file 3: Pirates and wreckers

The deadliest **pirate** of all time was **Blackbeard**.

His real name was Edward Teach. He was an English sailor.

Between 1716 and 1718 he caused terror in the Caribbean sea.

As soon as he appeared, other ships surrendered. If they didn't, the crew was killed.

Passengers were kept hostage. Blackbeard hung them if he didn't get what he wanted.

One woman passenger refused to give Blackbeard her ring, so he just cut off her finger.

He was killed in a sea battle in 1718.

Wreckers wrecked ships to steal the cargo. Many of them lived around the coast of Cornwall, England.

They lit fires on dangerous coasts.

Sailors thought the fires were lighthouses or harbour lights.

They steered their ship onto the rocks.

If the sailors weren't killed in the wreck, the wreckers finished them off.

Sea killers file 4: Tsunamis

Why do tsunamis happen?

- Underwater volcanoes.

- Landslides of rock falling in the sea.

- A meteorite or comet landing in the sea.

These things cause **huge waves**. In the deep sea the waves are small. People on a boat would not notice them.

When the wave gets in to shallow water the tsunami wave gets bigger.

The highest tsunami wave ever known was in Alaska in 1958. It was higher than the world's tallest building!

The worst tsunami for centuries was in 2004. Over 275,000 people died in South East Asia.

Mega tsunamis

Mega tsunamis are huge waves that can travel across oceans.

Scientist say there might be a mega tsunami in the Atlantic. They think a big landslide will happen in the Canary Islands. The tsunami would cross the Atlantic in a few hours.

New York and other American cities would be **destroyed**.

Sea killers file 5: Giant waves

In 1978 a ship called the Munchen disappeared in the Atlantic. It was one of the biggest **super-tankers** in the world.

The ship and its crew were never found. The only trace of the ship was an empty lifeboat. The disappearance was a mystery.

Many large ships like this one have vanished out at sea. People sometimes blame the sailors. Sometimes they say the ships haven't been looked after properly.

Scientists think the Munchen was sunk by a giant wave. The giant wave was not a tsunami.

Tsunamis happen on coasts. Giant waves happen in the middle of the sea. They can be 30 metres high. They can crash down on a ship and sink it.

Giant waves can even break a tanker into two.

How?

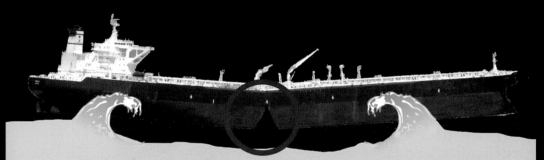

Two giant waves makes the tanker split in the middle.

What causes giant waves?

Scientist are not sure.

They think that sometimes waves join together, so one wave has the energy of a lot of waves.

They don't know how this happens. It might be because of unusual wind and tides.

Scientists use satellites to look for giant waves.

But still ships go missing . . .

Sea killers file 6:
The greatest danger of all – people!

Most deaths at sea are not caused by dangerous creatures or bad weather.

They are caused by people!

Why?

People can take silly risks.

- Swimming where it is dangerous.

- Taking a boat to sea without the proper equipment.

- Going to sea without proper training.

A really big mistake

In March 1989 an oil tanker called the Exxon Valdez hit the rocks. It was full of oil. Most of the oil was spilt.

The clean up cost two billion dollars.

How did it happen?

- The captain was not on the bridge.

- The man steering the ship had only slept for 6 hours in two days.

He forgot that the ship was on autopilot.

Coffin ships

In the 19th century, some ship owners put too much cargo in their ships. They did this to make the ships sink. Then they got the insurance money. If the crew died, that was just too bad.

These were known as 'coffin ships'.

Now ships have a line painted on them. If the line goes under the water, the ship is overloaded.

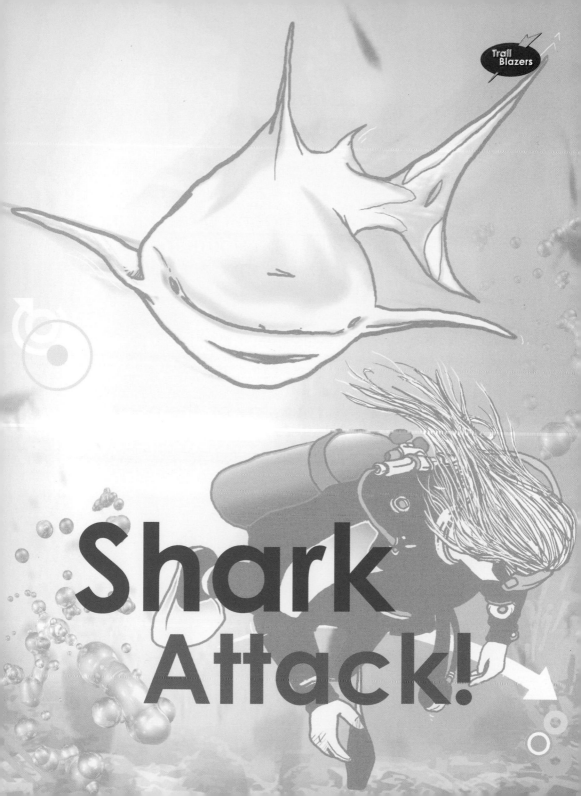

Shark
Attack!

Chapter 1:
The reef

Gary, Steve and Su hadn't dived for three weeks. There had been a storm. The sand had been stirred up. This made it hard to see underwater.

Now the water was clear again. The wildlife was great!

It was Steve's turn to stay on the boat. Su and Gary were diving. Su showed 'thumbs up' and they fell backwards into the water.

Su hoped the reef hadn't been hurt by the storm. But something had changed. They saw a dark shape.

A boat!

It was a small cruiser. Gary wrote on his board.

MUST HAVE SUNK IN THE STORM

What if the crew of the boat hadn't escaped?

What if there was a body inside the boat?

Chapter 2:
Coming their way!

They checked out the boat. There wasn't a body. Gary pointed to a rope. The boat had been tied up. The storm had broken the rope and the boat had been washed out to sea.

The cabin door was open. Gary swam inside. Su waited outside. It was a bad idea if they both went in. They could get trapped.

Gary looked round. It was a fishing boat. There was a pile of fishing gear in the cabin.

Gary heard something. Su was thumping on the side of the boat!

Gary started to go outside to see what the matter was, but Su was coming into the cabin. She waved her arms in panic. Gary looked over her shoulder.

A bull shark. A big one. Coming their way!

Chapter 3:
Smelling blood

Bull sharks were rare. Gary had never seen one before. It must have come in with the storm. Gary knew what to do.

He pulled Su into the cabin and shut the door. He put a finger in front of his face mask. Keep quiet. Keep still. The shark would lose interest and go away. It was midday. Sharks didn't feed at that time.

But then Su pointed at her leg. It was bleeding! Su had cut herself on something sharp.

The shark could smell the blood.

Su had cut her leg. The shark could smell blood . . .

It knew they were there. It rammed the door with its snout. Su and Gary went to the back of the cabin. Luckily the shark couldn't force its way in through the doorway.

How long would the shark stay there?

Su checked her air supply. Only enough for another half an hour. Then what?

Su's leg was only scratched. The bleeding stopped. But the shark didn't go away. The door began to break. Su and Gary could see the creature's staring eyes getting closer.

Would the shark reach them before their air ran out?

Chapter 4:
Hungry eyes and sharp teeth

The shark forced itself further in. The doorway began to break up.

Gary picked up a fishing rod. He tried to hit the shark on its gills. But the shark had tasted blood. Nothing was going to put it off. They could see its rows of sharp teeth.

Suddenly the shark jerked wildly. The water turned red. The shark stopped moving. Dead!

Gary looked through the window. Divers with harpoon guns!

Steve had saved them. He had seen the dark shape of the shark and had called the coastguard. The rescue team had dropped from a helicopter – only just in time!

Sea killers word check

air supply
amputated
Atlantic
autopilot
bridge
calm
coast
coastguard
creatures
cruiser
dangerous
deadliest
deadly
disappeared
dolphin
energy
equipment
extinct
harbour
harpoon
helicopter
insurance
lighthouse
meteorite

mystery
overloaded
owners
paralysed
pirates
poison
reef
risk
satellites
shallow
sound waves
steered
steering
super-tanker
tentacle
trace
training
tsunami
underwater
unusual
vanished
volcano
wreckers